USE ONCE AND DESTROY

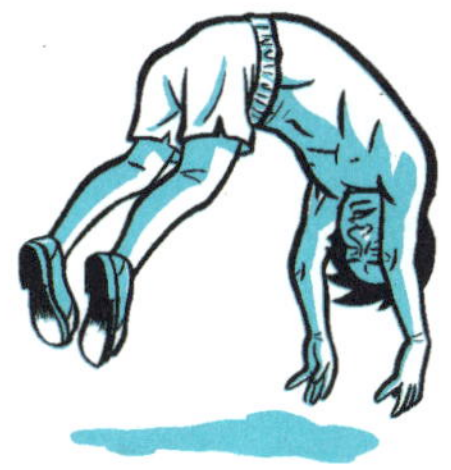

USE ONCE AND DESTROY

JOHN L'ECUYER

WITH ILLUSTRATIONS BY MICHAEL CHO

A PAGES BOOK FOR GUTTER PRESS
TORONTO

The publisher gratefully acknowledges the assistance of The Ontario Arts Council and The Canada Council for the Arts.

Canadian Cataloguing in Publication Data
L'Ecuyer, John, 1965 –
  Use once and destroy

A Pages book.
ISBN 1-896356-16-8

I.Title.
PS8573.E34355U83 1998   C813'.54   C98-930761-1
PR9199.3.L42U83 1998

A **PAGES** Edition of a **Gutter Press** book.
Published by Gutter Press, P.O. box 600, Station Q,
Toronto, Ontario, Canada M4T 2N4
voice: 416.822.8708, fax: 416.822.8709
www.gutterpress.com, email: gutter@gutterpress.com

Distributed in the U.S. and abroad by D.A.P.
Distributed Art Publishers, Inc.
155 Sixth Avenue, 2nd Floor,
New York, ny 10013-1507
To order, call 1.800.338.book
Represented in Canada by the Literary Press Group.
Distributed in Canada by General Publishing,
30 Lesmill Rd, Don Mills, Ontario

First Edition

Book design by Michael Cho
Cover Photograph by Chantal Fuller

Manufactured in Canada.

This book is for Marlene and Leopold L'Ecuyer for giving and saving my life over and over.

You don't need to know John L'Ecuyer personally to get an idea of the role hurry plays in his life. It's everywhere in his work. It's there in the cutting, camera movement and verbal torrent in his films, and now, with this book, the same breathless, breakneck velocity pumps through his prose.

Come to think of it, same goes if you do know him personally. Every time I talk to the guy — and we didn't meet until he kicked the old ways — he's whipping up another hellbent flurry of projects: movies, books, TV series, recordings, collaborations with people who hear the same music he does. You run to keep up with John, but he's always talking over his shoulder at you. Not that he's trying to get away. He wants you to come with him, it's just that it's his pace or no race. Likewise in his art: it's like some oven timer is always ticking in the storyteller's head, or he's trying to get everything out before whoever it is rounds the corner and slams him to the curb. Maybe he's worried about forgetting what it was he wanted to tell you, or remembering something he already forgot. Who knows. Whatever the reason, it's urgent. Always a rush.

An andrenalized memoir of his life as a junk addict in Montreal, **UseOnceAndDestroy** reads like a testimonial from someone trying to get it all out — or down — before he hits the sidewalk. To an extent, it's a familiar voice: it's the jangled junkie spew of the Beats and their literary progeny, of bebop and Lenny Bruce, of the new journalism and the old habits, the whole screaming rush to urban oblivion which is one of the most charismatic facts of post-nuclear literary life. Style, that is, but lifestyle too, which is what makes it so seductive and scary in equal doses. A line made for crossing.

Both in person and persona — the version of himself he's tinted for page and screen — John L'Ecuyer will tell you about the formative role romance played in his junk love: listening to Lou and the Velvets, air-chording with Keith, reading Burroughs and Carroll, getting completely low with Bowie and Eno in the imaginary Berlin which is the capitol of the country of pierced veins and seeping souls. The sweet soundtrack to dysfunction, the siren call of hip oblivion. Getting hooked on the idea of something cool and dangerous and out there and forbidden, then crossing the street from the idea to the act, where the cool turns cold and — spare me — the poetry of the experience means about as much as a spent syringe to everybody except the gullible, the uninitiated or the successfully flushed out. Like so much that seems romantic in life, it helps if you're not actually there.

Obviously, as someone who's been there and back, John is hardly alone in his public status as former junkie. Indeed, there was a moment or two during the odious just-say-no era — right about the time I imagine John imagining he's Lou Reed — when the righteous recovery testimonial was almost as common a talkshow staple as the opening monologue. In fact, it told you something of the climate's puritanical temper that you somehow seemed more deserving of your celebrity if you'd spent some of it suffering in rehab. Strangely, it was thus okay to have nursed a demon, just as long as you were willing to go on the couch and tell the world how bad and unhappy and sorry you were.

One of the bracing things about John's artistic excavation of his junkie history — and what makes it so compelling as a post-recovery alternative — is how unsorry he is. Or maybe I should say sorry for people who died or got otherwise lost, but not for anything he did. He chose the ledge, and nobody pushed him off. All that matters as far as we're concerned is that he bounced when he hit pavement, and that he wants to talk about what it's like to fall that far that fast. Maybe we'll learn something from it, maybe we won't. His job isn't to act as redeemer, but as reporter from the brink. To this end, he sees his history as technicolor-vividly as the words and images which spew in waves across these pages, and he wants to make sure we know the imperfect souls he met on the way down, many of whom are probably no longer there. It's his way of honouring their tarnished humanity, by talking up a storm about them before nobody remembers or cares anymore. Like trying to described the details of a dream before it slips away forever.

I guess that's one reason for the rush.

Geoff Pevere is the co-author of **Mondo Canuck: A Canadian Pop Culture Odyssey**, *published by Prentice-Hall.*

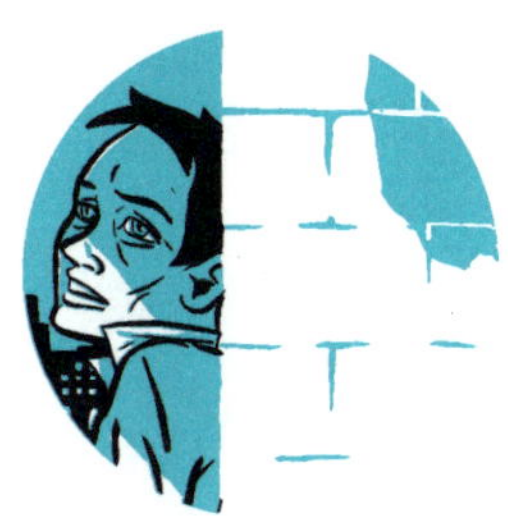

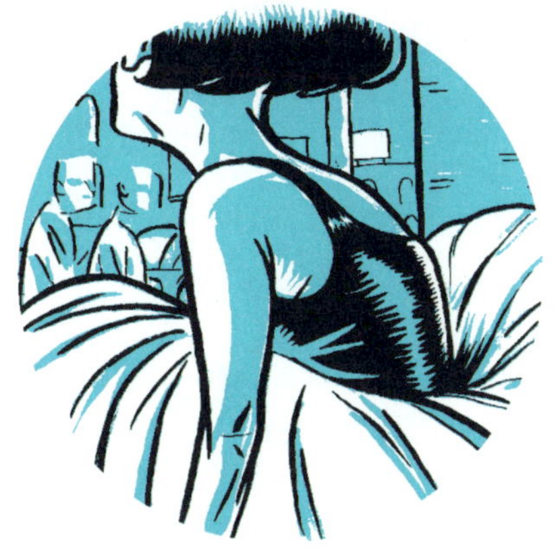

BRENDA

I met Brenda in a punk club when we were fifteen and all she wanted was to go-go and move all the time she couldn't stop she wanted to be seen to be noticed to fly to hover over all of us and at times she did and she never rested being the nervous adrenalized person that she was I mean she'd go-go all the time on the street on the phone alone at home wherever home happened to be on any given day. She'd wear those big fifties gowns that floated on her like a cloud of smoke until she'd kick it up in energized bursts that came from some demon within we met over and over again as we went our way and glued ourselves to bigger and crazier drugs and people and when I saw her again and again her dress got bigger and she didn't go-go as much or at least when she did it seemed more like a flashback or a yearning for simpler times.

Jimmi was her man she'd say and he didn't go-go but he'd strut and no one knew why because the few little bank jobs he pulled were no sign of success at least to us who spent time with him at our own risk but somehow that little guy was winning back something his father had beat out of him a long time ago with a rubber hose this is the truth I swear his father wanted his boy trained and strong but he turned psycho and wild and I liked him but he needed escape all the time he couldn't piss without starting an argument or planning to kill some fucking junk dealer for selling him short and of course he was as petrified as the rest of us but he bought the romantic Warner Brothers gangster image that held our brains together during the bad times and added atmosphere to the good he stole cars and I think that is all he really liked I mean he was strung out like the rest of us but it was the cars he really wanted and when I'd catch a ride and I mean catch a ride with Jimmi in his latest jag or vette we'd fly over other cars and through alleys and I'd feel good sailing along in the passenger seat wondering if we'd kill someone or ourselves and at the time we didn't care although there was one time on the highway when I was junk sick and needed to score and Jimmi decided to roll the car I wasn't all that happy.

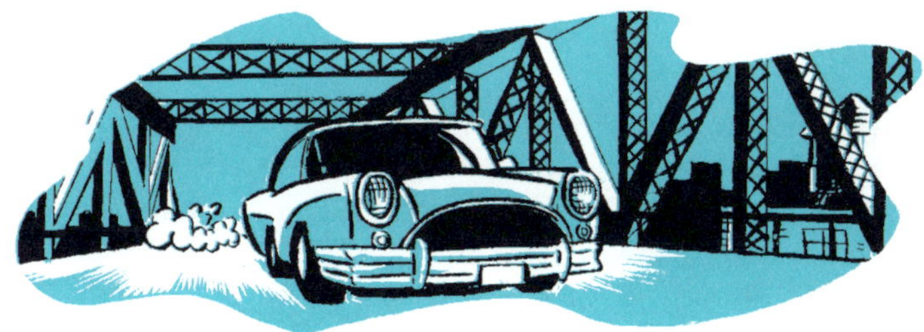

Brenda's dress got bigger and bigger and her arms got these big purple blotches and I never brought it up but I started to feel strange and every time I saw her I wanted to cry or had that feeling inside that something was wrong her dress got so big and she never go-go-ed anymore and I thought sometimes she'd disappear when I'd look at her and then Jimmi decided everything was too much and drove into the back of that grocery store and lit himself on fire which I swear is true but weird had I been Jimmi I would have driven off a cliff or something.

Brenda got sicker and it wasn't long before all that was left was a big dress and a little person inside with sad eyes the last time I saw Brenda was on the subway and she couldn't walk anymore and I sat beside her without saying hello or anything because she didn't recognize me and I realized that life was changing and taking on new meanings every second and I didn't like any of them.

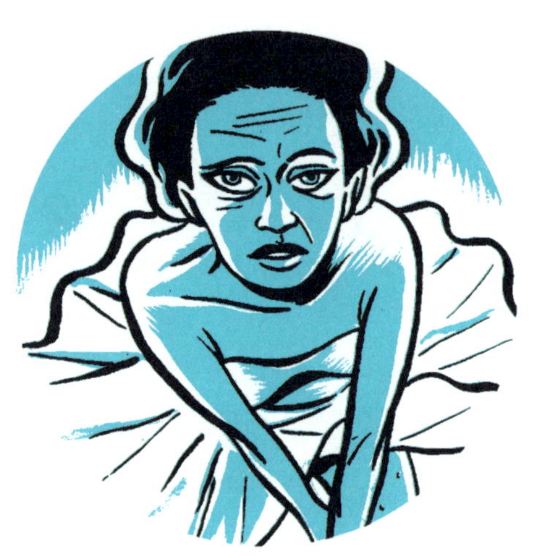

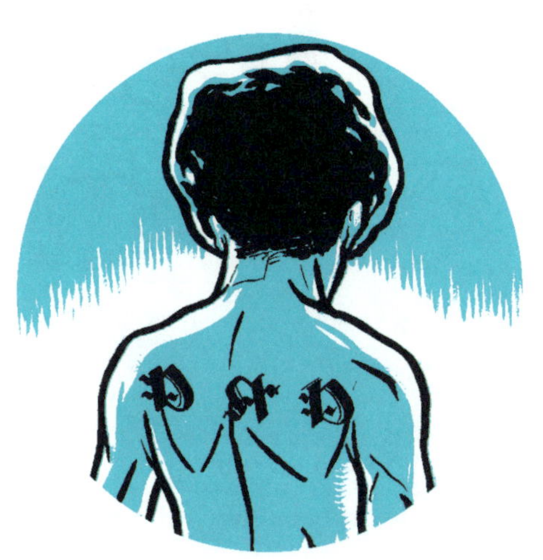
PAD

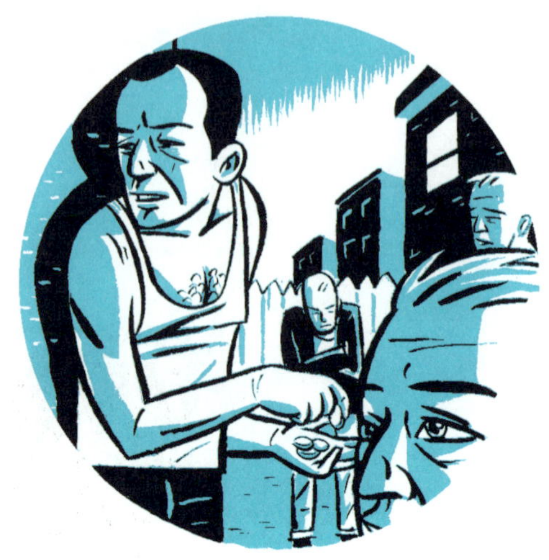

RED THEO

Red Theo was fat pale and smelled of flesh on those hot humid

days when I thought I'd throw up just standing beside his holi-

ness my dealer on one of those stinky wretch-filled days Red

Theo informed me that I could get a shift dealing in one of the

rat-infested hole in the door hole in the wall McDealerships he

was setting up so I started made money stole money got as

fucked as my brains and motor coordination would let me and

I was happy but one day while in the room I was trading dope smack for coke and started shooting jamming cramming ripping that needle up and down my arms searching for those fucking veins who were on to me and dodging my every stab coke smack coke took on its own life and careened out of control until my girl Nancy noticed me sleeping under the bed well not sleeping shaking and talking and eating Rice Krispies unable unwilling to get out I needed a break.

Red Theo called and knocked and drove by with menacing faces sending telepathic messages for me to get my shit together but I liked Red Theo don't get me wrong he believed in heroin like a religion praying each and every day and he took care of his flock like any good father would so who could deny him his right to threaten shiny pointed knives and eternal damnation to those he thought were about to sin.

I scored some pills a bag of downs and dropped them like candy
and ended up in some dream state on parc avenue climbing in
and out of taxis with drivers looking concerned in rear view
mirrors which if they only knew made me weirder and weirder
and fuck knows where I was going in such a hurry the cabby
sure didn't and finally I found a sweet smelling field and everything...got ...slower ...and ...breathing ... got ...harder.

I woke up to cars crashing and twisting around me and the
stink of exhaust in my eyes nose and mouth and some kind of
spider was having a family in my opened pants that some pervert worked down the night before but by habit I stood and fell
all the way to work.

White sunlight blasting through my lids I'm loose and dazed
and beat inside out with every step as the 9-to-5-ers divided
parted stopped and gawked and I think I told them to fuck off
but maybe that was the conversation I was having in my head
which felt like a little universe spinning and wheeling out of

control with my reality and the reality running parallel and at

the corner I met the first nest of hornets waiting for their fix

pissed off and sick sweating and the closer I got the more

fucked the situation grew there they were standing on the

stoop in varying states of junk sick some off the side doing the

faithful he's gonna get here soon I can feel it shuffle and others

forcing the issue peeking around corners and slinking around

pay phones like cats in a fight.

The pervert had the key.

The pressure of my sick little family and the left over delirium

propelled me up the fire escape like a monkey towards the

stash I knew was hidden beneath the floor they cheered from

below and for a second looking down from the fourth floor I

thought maybe I could let go and everything would be okay

again but their voices kept me on that thin line I needed to con-

tinue.

From the window I could see Red Theo pull up to the curb all calm and slithery soaking up his power as the congregation lowered their eyes and held their breath in awe of the man the spirit the deity this father our father my father whose feet never touched the ground he looked up at me with a gentle comforting accepting glance and I realized that I enjoyed this moment more than any other with my bloodless lifeless family below about to storm the door and regain their soul through the eye of a needle and Red Theo our pope looking on lovingly those moments when they work are family moments that left me with hope.

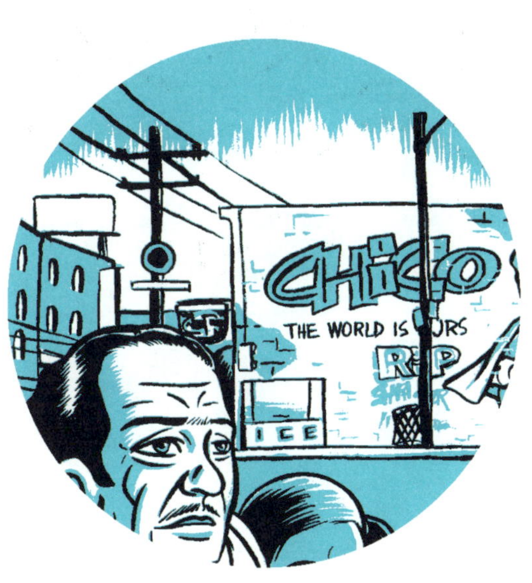
Chico
THE WORLD IS OURS
R.I.P
ICE

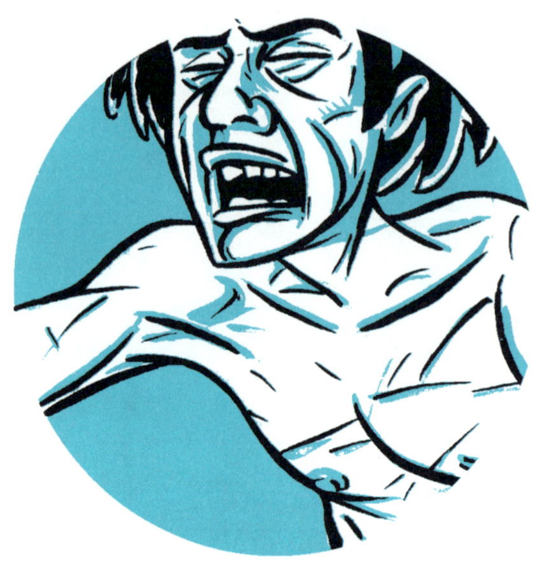

NICE GUY NELSON

Nice Guy Nelson's twisted jutting reaching dreadlocks were directly connected to the disturbed manic depressive brain that tortured him his whole life from the first suicide attempt at age nine from a 7th floor balcony which busted up his knee and gave him that funny limp to the razor blade phase that you're always reminded of because no matter where you look you see some scar gouge rip from some forgotten night when Nice Guy Nelson's brain was folding up and turning black and although I always looked at him through beauty tinted lenses I had to look away it hurt to see so much pain.

One day or the day to end all days had Nice Guy Nelson throwing in one hundred 222's three bottles of red wine and a full syringe to seal his fate but he ended up on a late night street corner spitting out ribbons of red and green and brown as horrified real people dodged and darted from this human fountain of disrepair.

So the wine didn't work but the pills would.

He woke up on the floor of a rooming house with again the urge to puke and shit he gagged violently with his pants around his ankles and his head in the tub with a panicked rooming house audience staring in at the freak show animal magically producing red brown and green liquid words from awful deafening screams and it was at that moment Nice Guy Nelson knew what to do to live so he sat back on the toilet and reached under to retrieve a clump of pills from his ass all covered in blood.

I was in a drug haze as usual and standing on the corner as usual when I last saw Nice Guy Nelson and from his mouth the usual I want to die I want to slash I want to burn music rang out and blended into the other sounds of the neighborhood as we walked he talked I shook my head but stayed focused on the melody and rhythm of the only song Nice Guy Nelson could sing.

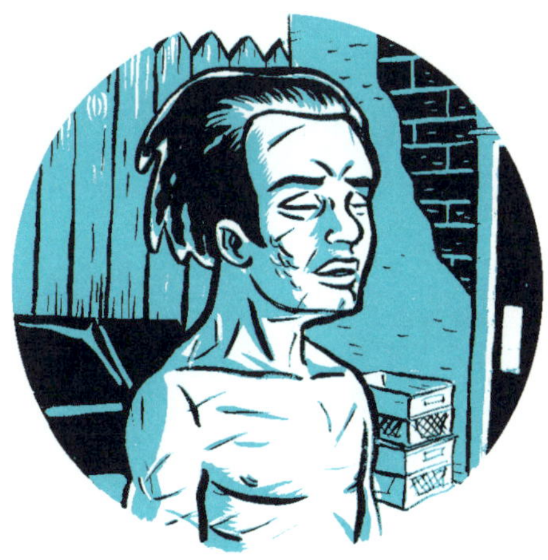

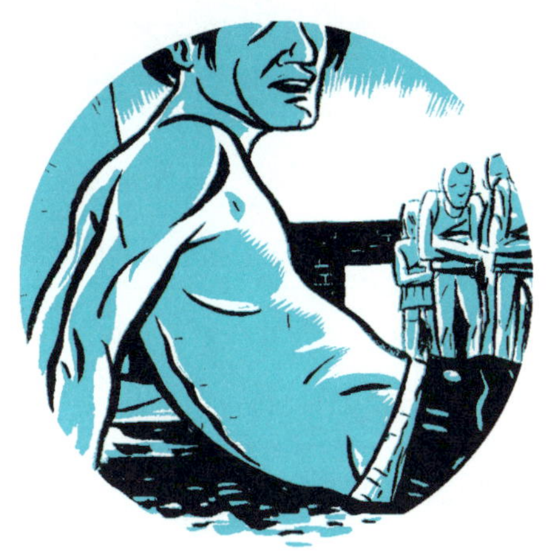

This is my first time here a harder blacker greek place on st. denis street that has guys with cell phones on the stairs and across the street ready to relocate us if there's a bust the climb is hard eight, nine stairs that feel like a lot more the door has a face inside I've seen before but never spoken to I claim famil-iarity parc avenue you know the poolroom Steve and Trifano oh yah c'mon in nerves and need help me along I'd rather not be here black white red rings of smoke floating over raised eyes

from the floor bodies look the same faces look the same eyes

feel the same floating gently upwards to catch mine I walk

close to the wall knowing relief is soon the cramps in my legs

remind me of why I'm here but its different desperate like

walking in water this place is like murder I dropped into the

end of the line then took time to pause to breathe to move and

I saw him dennis hanging onto some pissed off guys arm like

ripped fabric his face dented with shadows and lines penciled

in to give him life I was surprised and nodded my recognition

but his eyes swallowed my gesture where it was lost in a deep

empty pain.

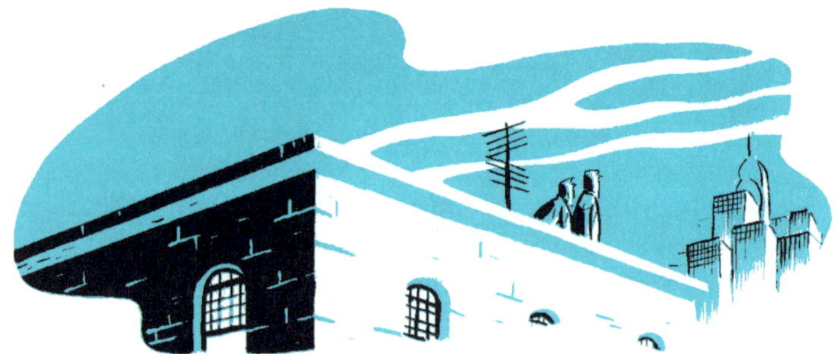

Dennis I knew long ago when we started this life he was born
like me but he was stronger and shorter and louder a lovable
beast needing to be heard with a beautiful angel for a wife with
winks and sly smiles she was sweet and knowing and laughed
away the fear he created for all of us so we stayed glued to her
a little family I was warm there familiar catching my reflection
in brown thoughtful eyes that reminded me that I existed to
someone else but he dealt beautiful white junk too and she
couldn't know she was pregnant but that's way too hard to
think about now cause he's tripping over everyone and
although previous respect bought him patience from a few I
could see that some natives didn't like seeing a mirror of our
future tripping over them with drool and disconnected arms
flailing about I watched him the shadow of Dennis raise his
arm his palm up and attempt slapping his own veins to atten-
tion a needle slid in without hitting and we could see even from
the end of the line a rising disgusting abscess that grew from
his abused mainline.

I could feel pain for a second my eyes and chest and heart tightened with his as he collapsed slowly to the floor and I kept thinking about his beautiful Angela almost like she was smiling away the pain for others who were witnessing a complete horrible painful body burn slowly from the acid of his self hatred I could see her understand and live it with him like it was what she saw in herself and for a second a sharp slash a pin or a knife cut through me tensing my fingers raising my shoulders spit fell from his mouth disgusting the younger boring the older we all had problems and we all were paralyzed from doing anything I tried not to look showing anything in this place was a problem.

The line reversed and a brown quarter hit my spoon Dennis now at my feet was watching a thin stream of blood run from the hole in his abscess it wasn't a living body face arms skin I could see skin that hugged the contours of his skeleton more than I had ever seen before even on dead people they called next I turned right grabbed a glass and set down my spoon at the edge of a glowing red ring on the stove my eye caught the

blood trickle from his wrist to his kneecap to the floor my hit

ready I study him as I tie up rolling my eyes down to my line.

Mixed blood disappears and when I look again Dennis has been

dragged away by muscle with a phone but the trail of blood led

down to some stairs where he was piled in a crumpled heap and

when I snuck down lowering my mouth to speak the stench of

rotting flesh washed over me his legs and arms had black rot-

ting patches his eyes were open I spoke but the words echoed

back having found nowhere to go.

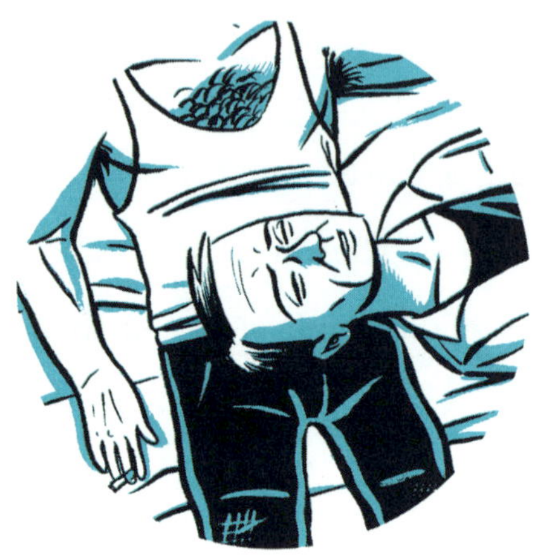

HARVEY

The way Harvey peeled down my pants made me laugh shimmy shimmy hum hum oh my oh my all to some sorta singing in
the rain shit .

The routine the dance the shirt flap hanging out the destroyed
doomed son of a bitch designed to drive fags into temporary
wives off hochelaga street where we meet with me playing the
hungry addict happy to see a cheeseburger apple pie close
enough to touch with fat rich grocery store Harvey wanting me

in his mouth the most I grew to see that I am addicted to everything heroin coke escape the long strokes of a deep throat on cold afternoons behind the dumpsters of the montreal poolroom in motels with names like emerald palace in family volvos breaking children's toys under my feet while their lie my lie the lies of everyone paused in private the first time my mind puked with the horrors of hell that were there waiting at the end I knew in my heart a time would come when we'd pay. I flew to other places needing distraction from the glide of my shaft moist riding his tongue like a girl rides a horse we are all motherfuckers little beasts desperate for feeling and love and hope and in that position we served a purpose my drugmoney his lonely throat our bonding rhythm that filled our eyes with fear wonder strange embarrassment and when I'd lose control and fill my heart into his with a strange tremor that was love.

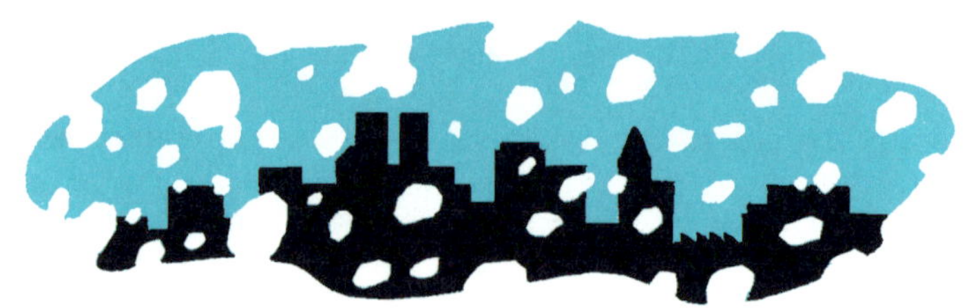

Harvey picked me up from court on a windy january afternoon my clothes torn each breeze reminding me of my flesh in disconnected flashes of small pain my brain left another judge doing his part maybe worried I'd recognize him but now the short walk to harvey felt long junk sick my bowels about to release the feeling I hate that grips your stomach and twists it inside out and all this was just another day hoping for a little pity a sleep that was warm with me watching the demons clawing at the window finally at safe distance he welcomed me "aboard" and extended himself to me but all I wanted to see were eyes of love and Harvey sure had those snow whipped around the van like those glass balls you shake up to remember innocence and I felt warmth wrap its arms around me like some kind of hallucination that you really want to be true.

We drove into white for so long while I smoked he smiled and something seemed peaceful slow real the van filling with curls of smoke and some hokey country music shit that made me want to cry from relief relief from sore arms and the aftereffects of that dope cut with some shit that made my piss red and my arms swell to twice their size I'll kill that peace of shit Andrew for dropping that junk on me when I was sick but he's probably worse off right now anyway.

After steak and fries and the don't-buy-drugs loan Harvey drove me past my rooming house as usual and I unzipped my pants as usual knowing that the day was short and I needed to score he reached over and squeezed my hand like a dying man would squeeze the hand of his lifelong love and I was awkward and unsure we stopped he pulled his funny ass out and when he returned he handed me the key to some motel room we'd stopped at. I got out he said goodnight sleep well.

I stood there stunned as his van disappeared into white.

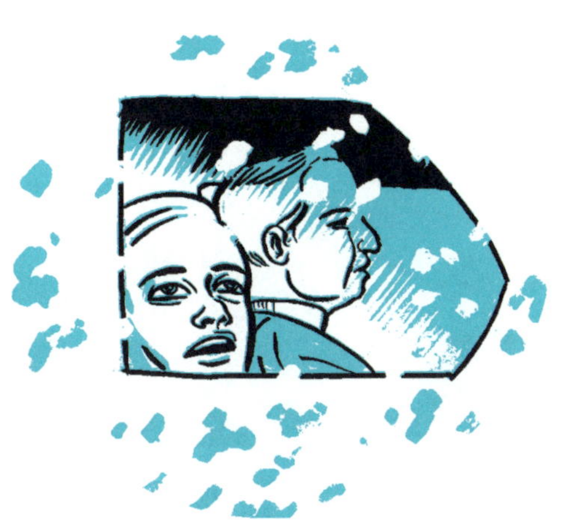

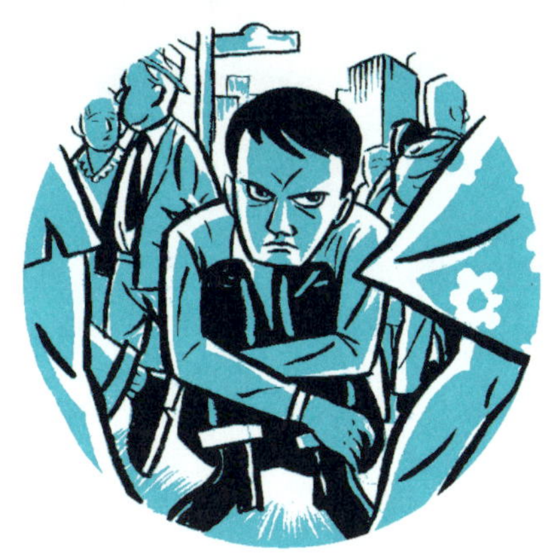

SPEROSUNDAY

Every sunday was do or die dog eat dog bite the bullet with hor-
rific cravings thirsts yearnings set against a bland relaxed lets
do brunch city background I am the gnat pestering hovering
unrelenting moneydrugsmoneydrugsmoney I am hyperfocused
a Buddhist in hot pursuit of chemical serenity although some
days unsuccessful days when my every pore pleaded begged
and screamed for divine intervention a helping hand from god

satan anyone with a little power for just a little roll of forgotten twenties in my path a dropped wallet beside the sports car on the corner a generous fucked up dealer or co-conspirator to aid and abet my nasty thoughts.

On those days when I scored in the greek neighborhood I believed I could will summon from the dead my gentle spero whose knife point sharp blue eyes had reflected deflected twenty thirty years of murderous intentions and quieted the I WANT THE FUCKING MONEY screams of dealers with shotguns for tongues and sparking circuits for brains spero was a prophet a comforter a lovable sleazy son of a bitch with lightning bolts of compassion for those of us who hung onto our hearts like so many helium balloons in a storm.

I met him and left him on the corner of mont royal and jeanne mance where the other spirits of junkie past hung out waiting for one last hit spero came from there nowhere having entered the in-between from a holding cell seizure from valium withdrawal that pushed him off the edge of my neighborhood map

but the corner of my eye caught him like a photograph that I

pulled out tattered and torn to reminisce about a time when

god walked the earth and taught me about life.

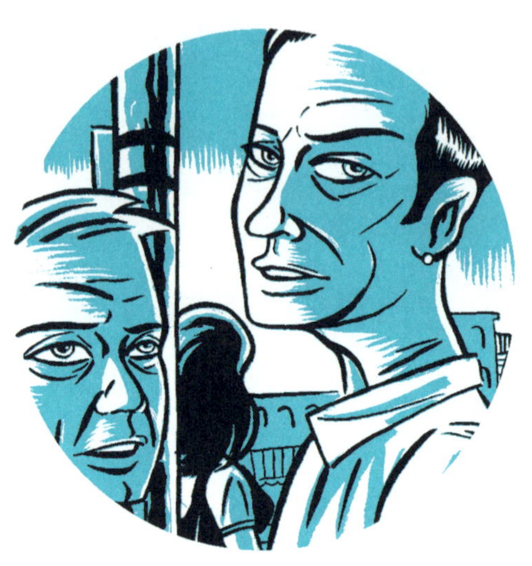

BOBBY DWAYNE DUSTYS AND DILAUDID

Dustys diner was home a chrome cockroach arborite wax museum where we the living dead would congregate for coffee well not so much for coffee but more for a sense of belonging a hard days work demanded a respite a safe haven to network lounge tell stories beg forgiveness and occasionally plead insanity. Bobby and Dwayne were smack users from long ago they grew up like me on their hands and knees stealing glances at scarred and chiseled champions of self destruction local heroes dark and cool easy and smart heroin was the fuel the motivation the church and latter day condom for mistakes like us self-medicating doctors on slippery streets and dimly lit alleys trading and stealing living and dying on a brown or white dust that healed for a while the torn bruised brains and forever struggling hearts.

On a perfect about to rain Thursday afternoon I was heading to Dustys when out of the gray I saw Bobby and Dwayne walking feet dragging leaving a junkie trail I pursued until my heels dragged along with theirs I asked the usual is it good how much where'd ya get it questions to which I received only pleasure filled grunts and mumbles that could only come from the mouths of those with chemicals for blood and brains that slam shut at the piercing point and push of a needle we dragged along looking ridiculous in our black suit jacket uniforms that hid the scars on those 93 degree days.

We were shadows amongst the crowd.

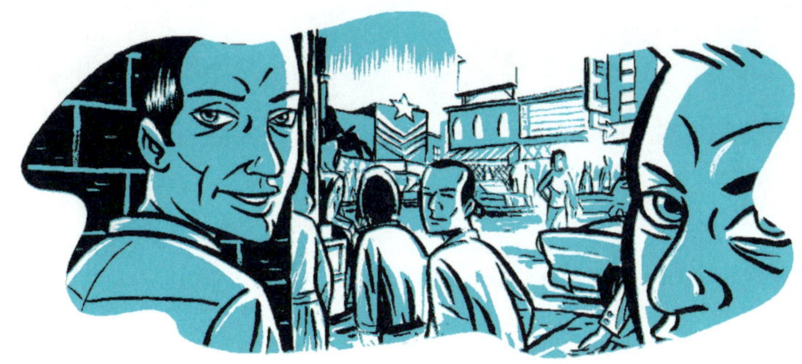

Dils man was all I understood from that sloppy and usually dancing mouth that Bobby used on people that mouth his contorted body slashing arms and trembling legs were a drunken ballet of cons cliches and out of this world but totally believable manipulations that never left his audience cheated it was art high art that people paid and paid and paid to listen to even though it was only used to cop a smoke or twist a bus token from the pockets of the naive.

His head turned in slow motion with his dirty hand rising from his jacket pocket to reveal a prescription bottle marked dilaudid now at that time it was dilaudid smilaudid to me but my hand rose to meet his the guarantee of its possibilities lay behind his and Dwayne's deadened stares we did the junkie haggle for what seemed to be hours until I scored and began my walk run flight to a corner garage station toilet to do up.

The rush hit me like a long orgasm that washed through my body up my spinal chord and nestled into the lower part of my brain leaving me stunned and content I leaned to the door and stumbled to Dustys determined to get more.

Lo and behold through the gauze of my vision in the first booth Bobby and Dwayne were weaving back and forth holding coffee cups close but not touching their mouths catatonic posing within the art of pleasure statues of inward escape.

I sat down into their dream for years leaving when my body decided it had had enough.

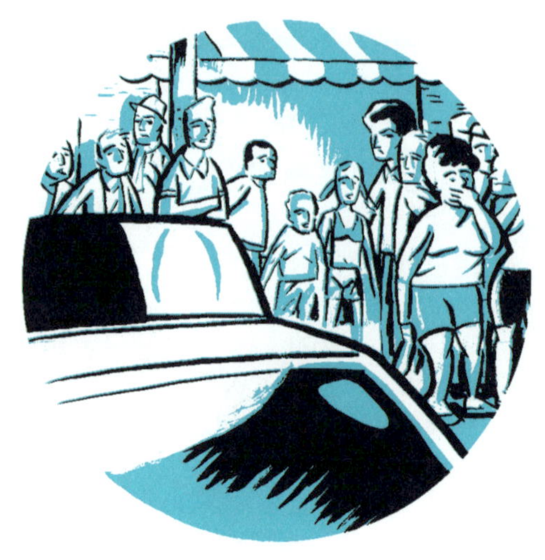

WHIRLIGIG DOUG

Doug was a dealer.

When I saw him I had to summon up little pockets of energy because even when doug was on the nod which was all the time the guy was spastic his arms and legs flew in every direction his eyes his pupils were like etch-a-sketch points that could never come under control or go where he wanted them to his whole existence focused in and around managing containing violently comical emotional actions and reactions his body shot out from within.

One day when I needed to score I hit Doug's place expecting nothing new just the regular but Doug was gone he was never gone you need to know Doug to understand that although he was a human whirligig his motion never brought him to the light of day he hid behind a New York Stop door with a sliver cut out as storefront periscope and oxygen source I swear that guy was packed in a chemical seal so tight I thought one day the apartment would suck into itself and disappear but Doug was ALWAYS there you never thought twice but now he was gone I milled about with others dumbfounded and disappoint- ed wondering where the eyes in the sliver went feeling the fear that one reserves for three legged dogs and blind people on dark killer streets.

We needed our fears panic settled search parties were organized after we scored elsewhere of course we began people looked everywhere I even lifted the occasional garbage can lid for some reason it seemed possible with a guy like Doug I walked for miles across the west side that on late summer nights felt like a horrorworld of howling lunatics and suicidal tendencies but all I found were the echoes of others pleading for the return of the eyes with the occasional muddled mugging or family firefight interrupting the shouts for Doug's return.

The day's light gained and I needed to shift priorities Doug was somewhere spazzing comfortably like the outta whack mother-fucker he was I thought so I went about the business of a new day hunting pecking scratching for money and dope I chased a bus up the street until I noticed a news truck on the side street there were flashing lights and people with fake concern on their faces I stopped not to gawk but because I received an invitation from the opened back doors of the news truck I was invited to pull out the video camera that lay there like candy for a starving fat kid easy money but as I waltzed back to the bus stop with my candy I looked back to see what was going on.

It was Doug, a frothing at the mouth ringmaster spinning out

of control on some poor bastards balcony.

Doug was a star.

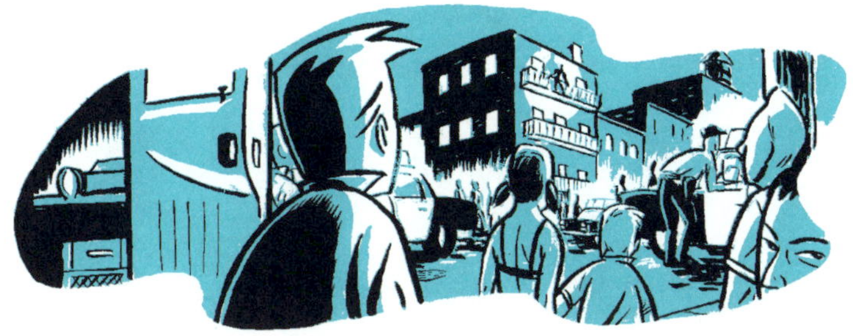

I stashed the candy and headed back for the spectacle it was

Doug's big break he was being born into the world he had self

aborted from long ago and I know that life mother nature the

gods would eat him alive it always eats the crazy deformed

young one way or another but I had to see.

He was screaming raving ranting his voice was hoarse and

almost gentle by this point and although it was difficult to understand through the gob filter and shouts of the recently arrived cops who were still in their pajamas and kissing their wives good-bye mindset I could see he had a gun or something his words sounded like a wounded animal and within me past the layer of sick human freak show curiosity I felt stabbing pain the kind that comes from life's strangeness the insanity we constantly try to understand and redeem like famine or murder

Doug was dead along time ago I know that from personal experience but something had welled up within him it was the drugs turning over in his brain and lashing out one more time to leave their mark.

Doug was immortal.

In one fell swoop the cops landed feet first on poor Doug who turned to dust and blew away no one noticed that but the cops and me as they cuffed him they thrashed his lifeless body around as if to demonstrate the danger he had been to the normal audience he had entertained but a minute ago his body poured into the cruiser while the cops laughed and congratulated their annihilation of the last of a species another kink in the carpet had been pulled out.

I returned to the candy and my own search for another day's immortality.

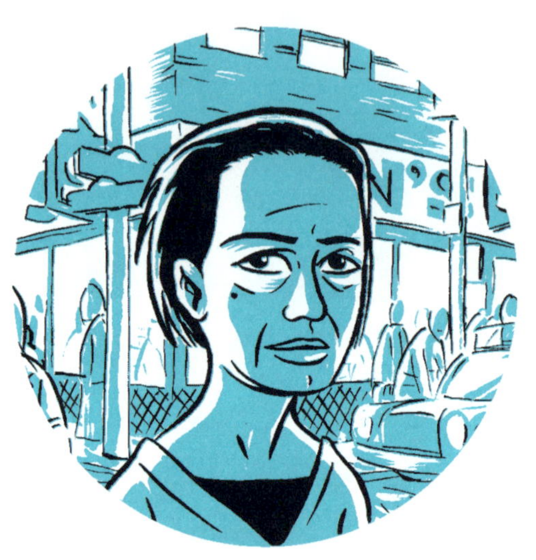

BLACK EYED SOPHIE

I fell far into Sophie's deep black eyes without ever speaking to her. She: small raven haired angel drifting into my scene afloat on damaged wings Me: a grey ghost of hepatitis and malnourishment focused on everything but life and living — she carried me from the scene for a few hours without saying a thing she just looked through my eyes and down to my heart and embraced it desperately as though one of us was about to check out from life and we both needed affirmation that we exist now and that we really were alive.

I: needed to score and that was the preoccupation always but She: was so intense that I had to feel her in the periphery of my vision and she caught the edge of my frayed and empty heart like a warm caress. Sophie glided with me along parc avenue Me: rabid and in need She: heavenly and bare we waited out-side bobby and johnny's GIRLS GIRLS GIRLS strip club for a never-ending length of life for dope so that I could once again slip into that cloud that let me see life without feeling a thing. She: A flashing red and blue lit dead beauty that stared with understanding and hopelessness all at once.

We never spoke and I knew nothing of her — not of her life desires or loss but I felt her penetrate me in some other way that I will never forget.

I think of Sophie often. I hope you are alive. I hope you are happy.

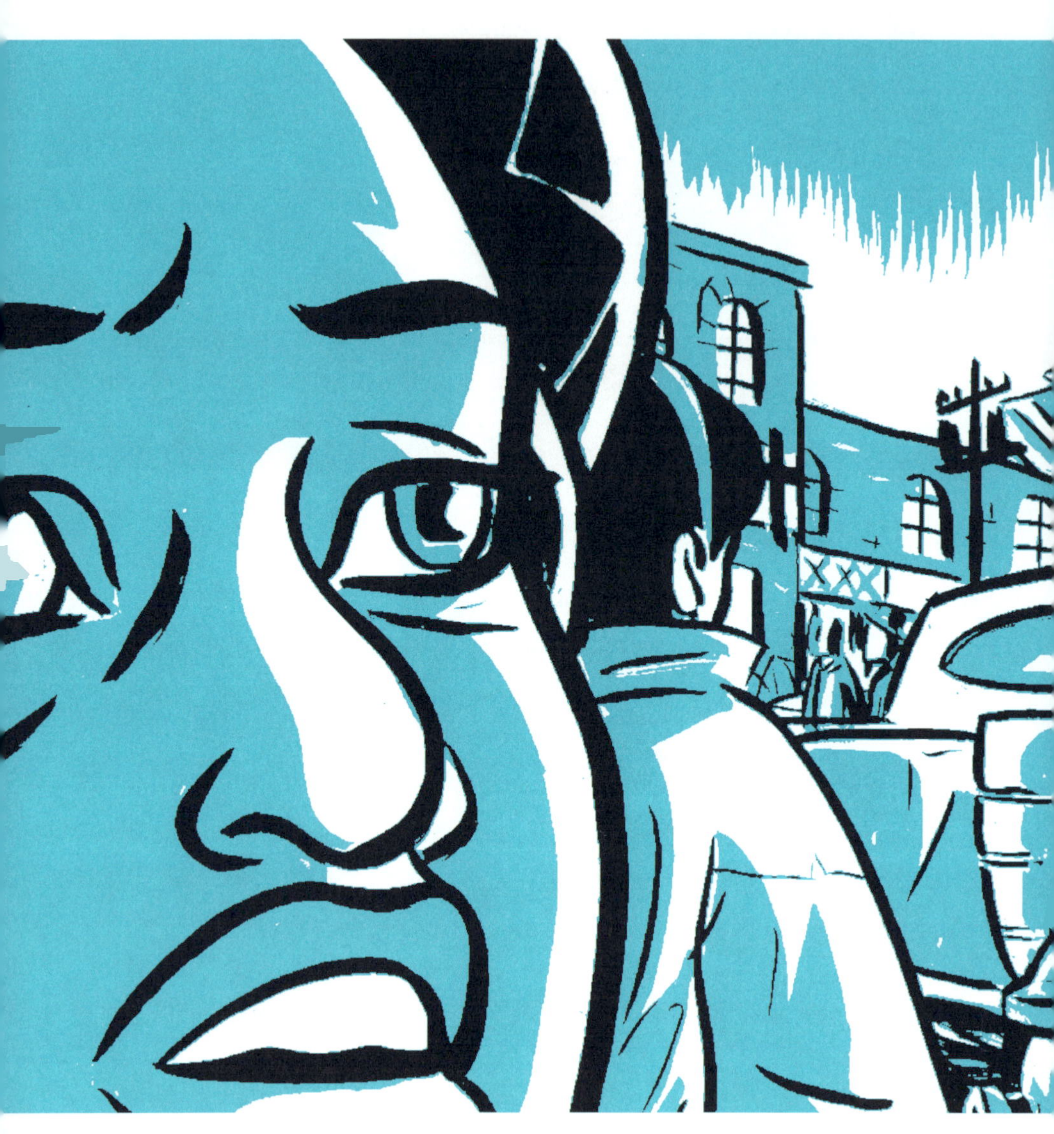

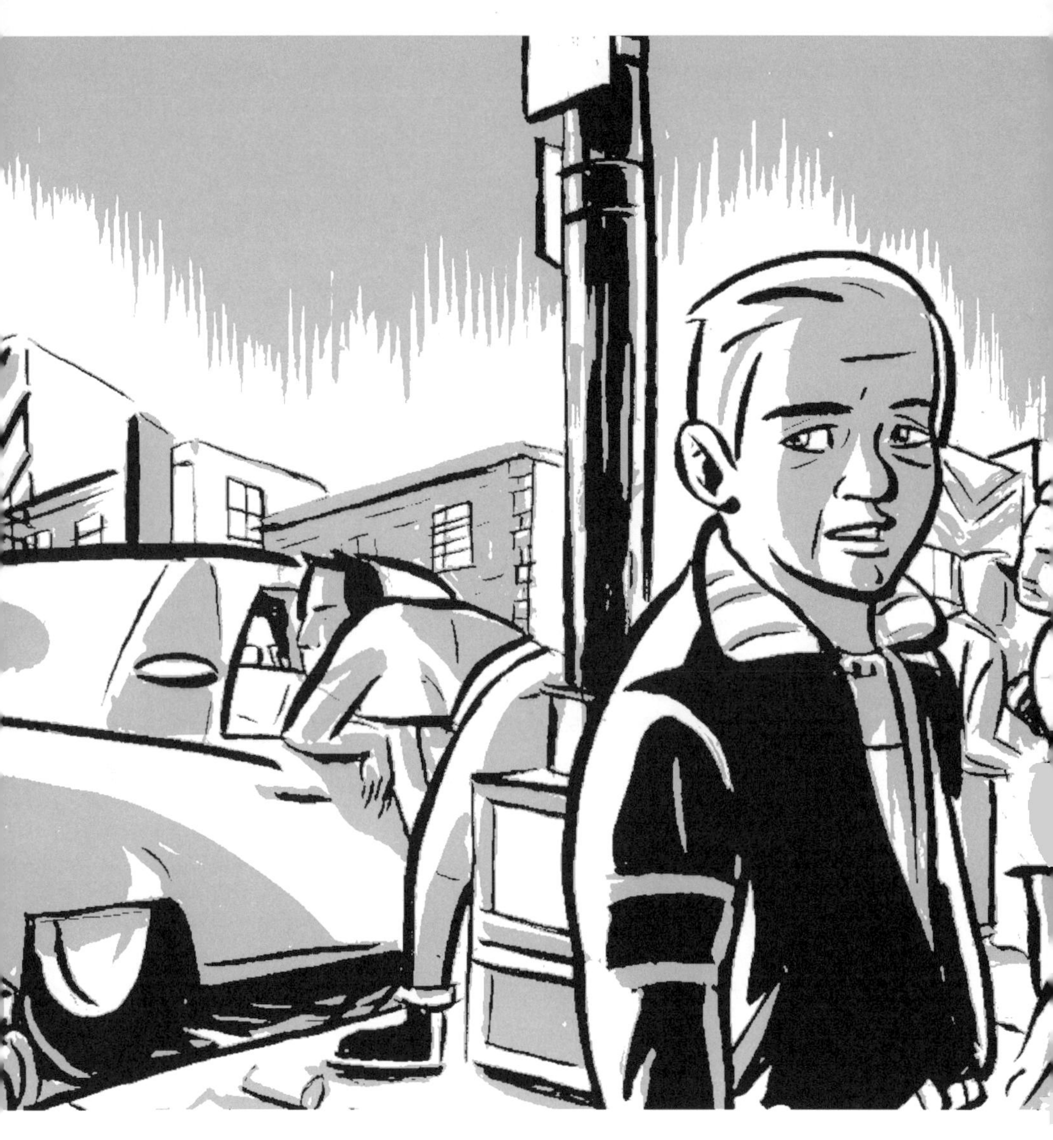

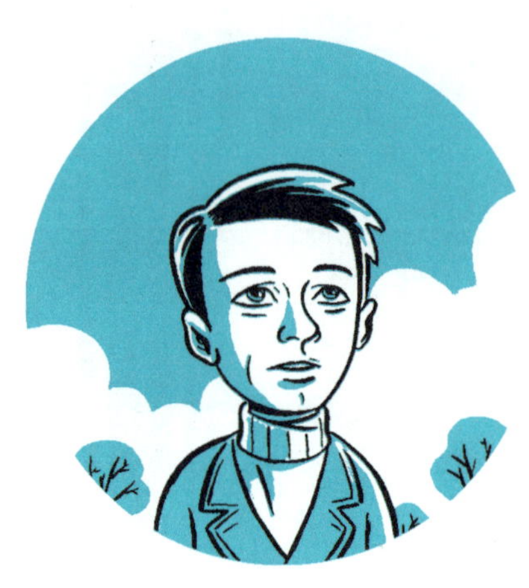

MY STORY

WHY

I do it to be free of the little tortures in my mind: the shaking anxiety, the wild-eyed fear, the black depression that clouds my vision every day, every hour, every minute. I know I'm incapable of totally escaping the demons within me, the demons that sing of silent blackness that is always, always the option.

I thought my reflection was the same as anyone else's until I grew up and over and over again I saw that I didn't fit in — I thought I was grotesque in appearance and people laughed in the breeze they felt as I scurried past like the rat I was. I spun a sort of anorexic's – auto mutilator's self-image out from within myself so that it sprayed everywhere. I felt my heart clench, freeze, and then burn

hot as others, I thought, judged.

My eyes found freaks, punks, weirdos, and others that acted like I

felt in my soul — an angry mutated misfit that wanted acceptance

more than any other thing. Real or imagined, my self-hatred was

what I *felt* — it was my truth.

But it wasn't always this way. I grew up like you wondering why

and understanding nothing until life was a pattern and destiny had

me in place. In my mind's eye I see a child, someone looking beyond

me like the look of a person a moment before the accident happens.

Heroin took me away from there, my darkness, and allowed me to

see the world for everything that is beautiful and crazy at the same

time — nothing could or would hurt me or so I thought.

Heroin isn't something I chose to do just like I didn't choose a lover

or make a friend — it was there for me, I was built for it and it was

built for me, like a cat knows when you've got a threat in your eye,

it was all instinct. I knew from the age of eleven that it was my destiny, although I knew nothing about it other than a few songs — self-
hating audio christ Lou Reed — desperate sad dying-with-every-
note Billie Holiday. I wasn't unsmart, I knew that between the
lines, woven into their lives' subtext was my soul and the souls of
others who never needed me to explain leadened blood because
theirs was just as heavy. I hate pity just as much as you, everybody
feels pain and its effects are always relative so it makes no differ-
ence who felt more or less, you know. What matters is that some of
us can't bear it and try to fold up and turn black right under your
feet.

A KID

Little teeth behind a smile that really hides the tangle of confusion
of the surroundings smashing me, drinking, arguments, unhappy
centers of my universe that drank in despair of incest, angst, bad
love, disappointment. Someone suffering from broken dreams kills

me so hard, I cry thinking about it. Everything doesn't work out and back when my eyes showed some vestige of purity tears welled for the intense sadness of my bearer, my beautiful family. When you love, really love, you die a thousand deaths for their pain. Who created who?

I'm running away from the things you say.

VALIUM AND BARBITUATES

I needed excitement and I needed it bad — I was eleven, man enough and big and bad enough — I cocktailed every pill I could. My friend Larry had stolen a syringe but we were too scared to use it, instead clouding our heads with dope chemicals and the occasional birth control or diarrhetic pill that only added to the thrill of Russian Roulette pill popping. We loved it — it was our world, where laughing and puking were okay in fact necessary to show just how cool we were to the others. Back then I mixed up looks of disgust with awe.

FIRST USE

I designed myself for access to the netherworld that had snakes with feet and people holding onto their retreating souls in desperate last ditch attempts for salvation before they'd murder themselves or someone else. I think black, I wear black, and when my eyes matched I was let in to the world of escape. I still remember the tip of a prepared syringe, a drip of junk forming in a display of innocence that smirked and let slip its true killer intentions. A flash — outside of myself I saw my curious look, like I almost understood this was beautiful evil. I looked away as my friend the fiend blindly jabbed it into my arm, the plunger pulling back, a little bit of me swirled into the syringe, mixed blood, paler looking, gentler looking, deceiving me like the rose with thorns it was. My fiend smiled "welcome to everything" as he pushed the plunger in and my body cascaded downwards to the depth of my soul — my heart flooded with warmth, orgasmic sensations that stuck around long enough for me to feel my mind open up and rejoice at the freedom it gave me to be.

HOW I FELT HIGH

High is my soul lifting out of me and standing over, gazing — the same curious look I used when I first met my killer. I cried inside I think, this is all I have now and everything around will rot for want of the real me to be part of the struggle along with them — lovers, family, friends are now just possessors of the colored paper I need to trade for a powder that I will push, force, jam into my brain every four or five hours. At first this was all okay with me. I blossomed, I fucked myself daily with the greatest, ego–boosting, confidence–giving mistress a man could ever want, feel, see in all of time. I floated down St. Lawrence Street, my head twisting in slow motion, seeing everything for the first time, unimpeded by my self- hatred. My cloud rising above the city I owned (temporarily), my vision losing the riff raff of you, all I can see are beautiful rats like me scurrying to and from taxis and shooting galleries yearning for the soothing chemical arms of their powder lovers.

I — I am Jesus fucking Christ Buddha God love orgasm with the forever feel of warm lips washing over my cock. You — you look at me funny when I pass, pulling your purse tighter and diverting your natural look and curiosity.

Sometimes I thought I could see inside myself as the drug careened through my veins, bouncing through corners and overwhelming my blood, my heart and my mind in a beautiful aggressive wave of perfect perfection. You never felt this good. I know that.

I want more and more and more and more. I start combining bittersweet smack with shootable coke sitting in bathrooms flushing the toilet over and over again, the tinny squealing distorted sound of the water coursing through the pipes grabbing the edge of my ears and swirling into my brain providing the soundtrack for my ecstasy. I could stay til I die but everything runs out at some point and I gotta get more.

I'll do anything, anything for money. At first it wasn't so for every dollar I spent came from selling my art, my possessions, next came my ass but that hurt as you can imagine so I decided — argued and convinced myself — that the world owes me something and I'm gonna take it no matter what. Of course I reconcile my guilt with strange unreal promises to God that I'll make the bad I do now better later besides they don't need CDs, books, their purse, if they only knew how painful withdrawal is they'd throw me the money as a humanitarian act. Sometimes though they got mad and I really didn't understand — don't they realize it is just as easy to kill them as to just steal harmlessly? They don't know who they are dealing with.   I was a rabid tazmanian devil, I was no longer responsible for my actions except to that fat cop from station 10 who thought I was, the bastard.

Using using using I go forever stretching the boundaries of acceptance from friends and always tempting insanity to come and take hold of me as a relief from the cycle I live. Morning is the quaking of my bowels ready to rocket out the alpha bits from the night before. Sweat, anxiety, shaky needy drug yearning make visions of theft, manipulations, killing for colored paper come to technicolor life. Crazy thoughts, atrocities born in my mind that shock even me — I see myself jumping the teller's counter and dislodging a bullet from my glock through the eyes and into the skull of anyone in my way, I see my baseball bat crushing the face bones of my devil dealer, I see my euphoric mind and body blasting blissfully into the sky from explosions I create for you.

If suicide is murder turned inward I'm gonna suicide a lot of people before the day is old.

I use my life's energy to clean and dress. The mirror reflects eyes like saucers and skin like paste. Don Juan Junkie. I hit the sheets of rain on St. Lawrence and parc avenue scanning everything. I am hyper-alert knowing that money is everywhere I just got to turn the right stones. I need a performance that arouses the sympathy of the hardened. A loan from a friend with high tolerance for people like me. I act calm as they open the wallet — red and brown would be fine but green suffices. I calmly exit and as soon as I'm clean I catapult myself across town, Parc Extension. Knocking hard the door opens to the womb I fight to return to everyday. The devil inside smiles a toothless grin we exchange inane pleasantries as though we really cared. Me and my mind: give me my fucking dope! The Devil: I give it to you when I feel like it.

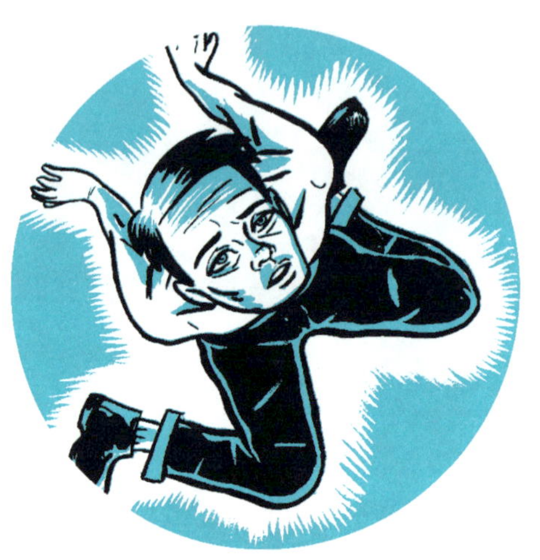

THE EXCITEMENT

I am so strong so cool so undefeatable I don't need you I don't feel hate I don't fear anything I am an electric charge for everything that I do. Screwdriver scratching into a car door lock I sit making the ignition connect to my brain. I am above everything I am power personified I own everything. The car is faster than it can sustain but everything is all right, I am already dead, catching that curb that throws me onto two wheels is no problem, those funny looking pedestrians are for dodging anyways I just know nothing will happen like I've seen it all happen before — I've leapt into the future, and saw myself on parc avenue 120, 140, 160 flying, sailing, outrunning reality. I ram the back of a slo-hog in front. I see their eyes ricochet off the rear view like bullets of fear and anger but I am bullet-proof I rule the world. Remnants of a conscience hold me on the thin line between murder and suicide — I'm too busy to have anything come to an end right now.

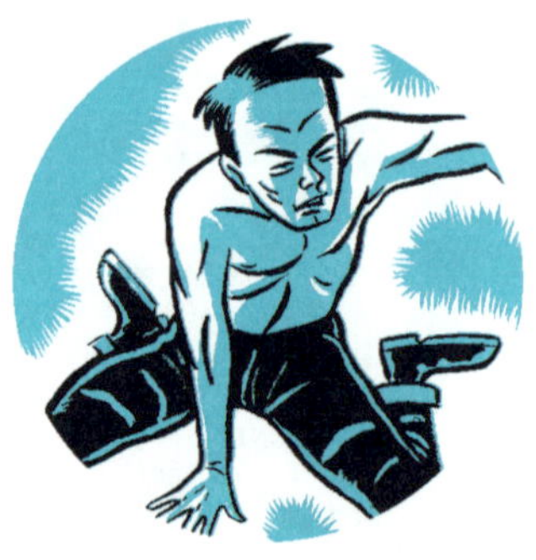

THE GAME

I pound pedals through an alleyway with a bag of dope in Snowdon

with a jerkstart – jerkstop – jerkstart grumbling cruiser with razor

edged teeth clumsily taking tight corners. My heart races I'm run-

ning away so hard. I push the bike forward while looking backward

I smash into a dumpster but adrenaline and heroin medicate me

always. My vision is bionic one foot after the other throws each

pedal down six feet into the ground and back up, I am a machine of

power my wheels are dancing feet of fear and excitement. I think to

not sweat too much in case it slithers into the bag and ruins the

dope. I look back at two headlights stuck behind the same dump-

ster, I stop, look back to reflect while bathing myself in red and blue red and blue red and blue darts of arcing light. I drop the bike and walk onto the main street telling myself to be cool think about baseball. Another cruiser drives up to me on the sidewalk — base-ball baseball baseball. They look at me and I slowly turn, acting the role of regular everyday man, and they creep away but not without the cops' hate–you stare. I'm fine, everything's fine.

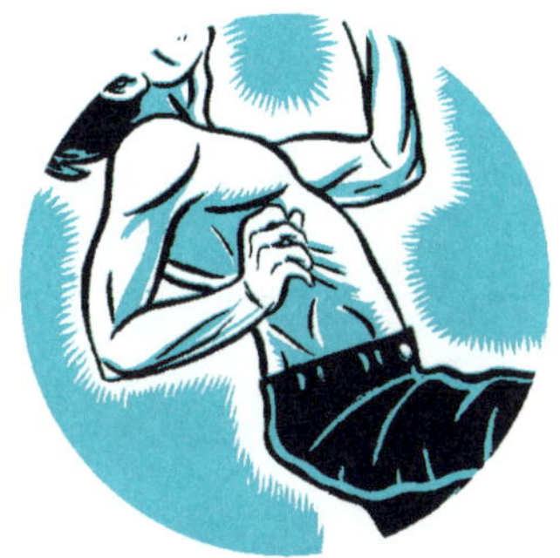

12 GAUGE HEROIN RECOIL

I am in a dealer's den. I want my eyes to look like killers from the slot of a ski mask. A bloody sofa in front of newspaper windows, Jimmy and Paul do the dirty work — ripped phone cords and gaffers tape fly like ribbons in the wind, sharp–edged knives caress an adams apple, fear and anger smash together to form perfect adrenaline. My view is of distorted edges a wide angle slowly rising to the ceiling. They fight back — Jimmy is kill kill kill and I love it to death, I am invincible. A steak knife lands in the assholes' thigh — did it happen? It feels like it did — after a second of serious realization, he shrieks like a dropped baby. I feel murder that works for me — money and dope thrown into a pharmacy bag — threats fly all over the room, bouncing off the walls and ceiling I see them dart by — revenge, death, the usual meaningless gestures. We leave with more but minus the knife. He can have it. We bolt through the corridors of wafting curry as doors open behind us and we laugh uncontrollably.

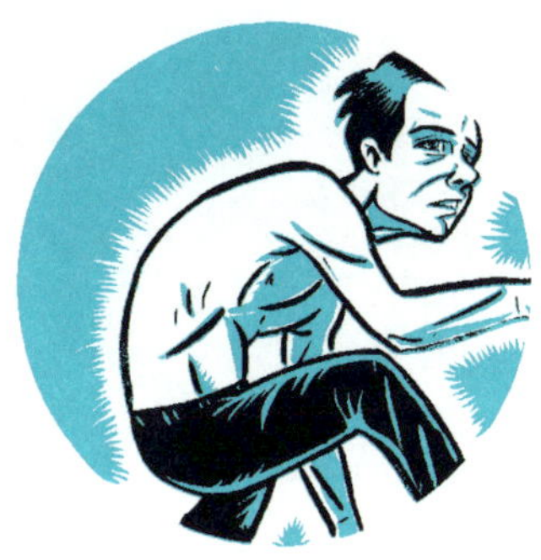

FIXING UP

I scramble from the Kaposi's sarcoma–scarred dealer's finger–tip-
ping of the scale to weigh out my purchase and head straight for the
already glowing coil on the stove; my spoon, my fit in hand are
strategically juggled, fit crossing my mouth giving a gauge–num-
bered smile while the spoon hits the counter. Water in a glass is
pierced and ripples out concentric rings of tainted water (a thousand
piercings that day). I pull back the worn white plunger, sucking
water into the chamber. I can almost hear it hit the black rubber at
the end of the plunger. My cigarette is ripped apart at the filter for
the cotton that is needed to stop the impurities that sneak through
anyway creating blood clots or cotton fever. I open a 1x1 folded piece

of lotto 6/49 that contains the drug and I let it carefully slide into the spoon; water follows creating a clouded concoction that I swirl with the tip of my fit, pushing the cotton in semicircles respecting the edges of the spoon. My heart pounds, a quiver down my spine — relief from the aching, anxiety-filled beginnings of killer cold turkey that is so close — I place the spoon on the ring, expertly heating the mixture to clarity, and then suck it up. I hold it up to the cupboard sky and tap the tip allowing an air bubble to gently dislodge from the centre and rise to the top. I gingerly push the plunger slightly, pushing out the bubble and releasing a drop of pre-cum to balance on the tip — I lick it letting its bitterness open over the tip of my tongue, a naked kiss. I rip my belt off hard and in one motion it coils around my thirsty arm, pulled tight my veins leap out fighting screaming to be the one. The needle slides in, vein bobbing slight-ly from side to side until it is locked in place by the piercing point of the metal tip. I slowly suck my blood back, watching the moment — cartoon stars throbbing out from my arm, little birds ready and set to chirp around my head — the plunger is pushed in and a second passes when I look at the ceiling, a strange unreal second in between the inbetween world of heroin. A wash of perfection laps over me — my shoulders lower an inch, my heart gasps, my legs weaken beautifully, the door slams on the approaching demons and I sail on a magic carpet through dreamy, lazy white clouds hearing only my pounding heart and John Coltrane. God and I are one. A few minutes of paralyzed nirvana pass and trumpets sound: I am alive again.

I float down the street. I love you and you and you — God has been renewed and you are all my lovers. The sky is grey and the air no longer chilling and crawling my skin. I see the good in everyone while walking through vignettes of life: hookers on the runway of lower St. Lawrence, cops throwing envious hateful looks at me from slow–motion cruisers, old people in bus shelters frantically chasing their slipping, escaping souls. I am an untouchable prisma–colour divine alien in the terrestrial world and it all makes me laugh.

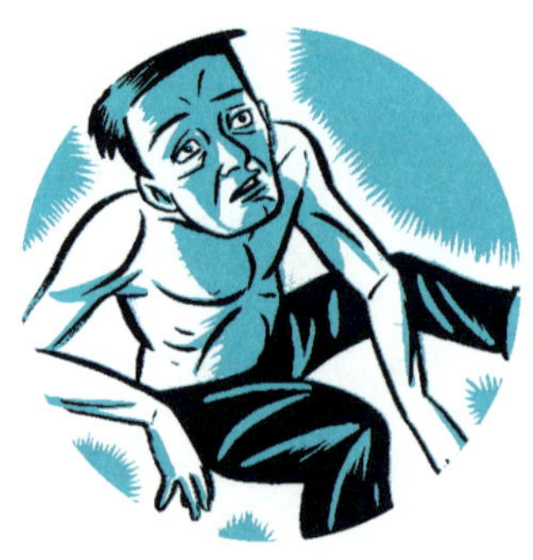

THE PANIC

Cops are laughing as I am let into the dealers' den; another sweep by our finest leaves my pack panting and thirsting for a dealer with drugs. After a shakedown by the righteous mustachioed I return home to face the inevitable: the bed is wet with my blood sweat and tears — what goes up must come down. My guts ache and will expel everything from any available orifice. My legs throb my spine twists my head is desperate, popping images of bathtubs and razors, guns and night tables, ropes and ceilings, but instead I lie and writhe, twist and turn, letting my melting soul grumble out low moans like an angry about-to-fight cat. Minutes are like hours that turn into years. Masturbation gives a quick second of relief but I'm emptier than before — my body rots before my eyes as I transform from deity to the sick warmth of the puke piss shit baby I am.

Three days pass and every second is sketched into my mind like a vampirella comic.

I re-awaken from being too awake and I am back to normal. I stand, a little shaky, it's been so long since I felt my feet touching God's own floor. I awkwardly pull on fresh clothes; the sensation of cotton brushing over my chest, nipples, and back is irritating and strange.

I move outside and the sun is like bleach in my eyes and peels the final layers of skin from my reddened face. I don't like this very much. Too much raw banal reality.

I don't last long because the cycle of my addiction still has seven years to go.

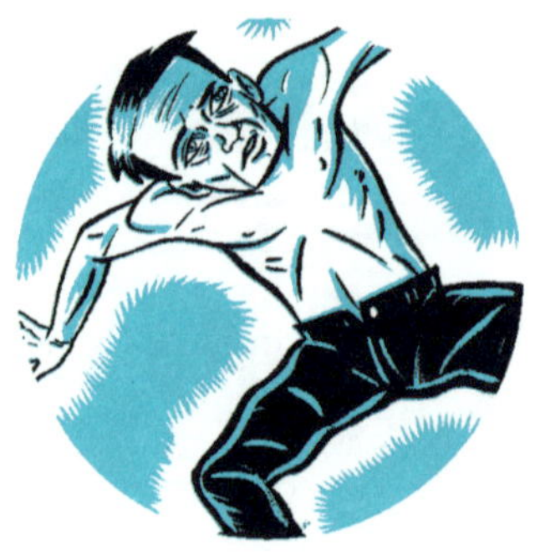

NARCAN AND ME

OD-ing is funny. I scored some extra bitter extra beautiful extra fantastic brown Iranian heroin on Clarke street and I hit home with good intentions — things were good, money drugs money, no need to cry these days. I did my hit and felt fine, real fine, fine for more and shot extra into me. My head responded good at first but then I started to fly out of control. I remember the cold tiles on the floor as my breathing feels labored and my heart has to summon all it's got to keep my blood crawling through my body.

The motion of a gurney ripping though a corridor, the breeze I see but can't feel. My bed is rubber as a smiling distorted doctor leans over me, my clothes are being sliced by a nurse, I feel a second of love but that drifts like everything else. Cold gel on my chest and little suction cups. A needle dances into view and I willingly stick out my arm to receive it like the old habit it is. A moment passes and I wait to feel good but it doesn't happen. I look up at the doctor who's got his hands weighing down my shoulders and I feel something surging inside me — I think I don't like this — my heart speeds and my stomach buckles — vomit shoots out violently, my skin crawls so painfully I am going insane, I'm crying begging for mercy I can't take it any more kill me kill me kill me! It won't stop it gets worse and I puke harder and harder and harder my eyes are popping from their sockets I scream ripping the suction cups from my chest, the walls part as policemen laugh in a chorus. I am insane the doctors are laughing the nurse is laughing as they torture me to death from my inside out. I am covered in puke and shit. As they pick me up I am crying please please please save me, and spin into darkness.

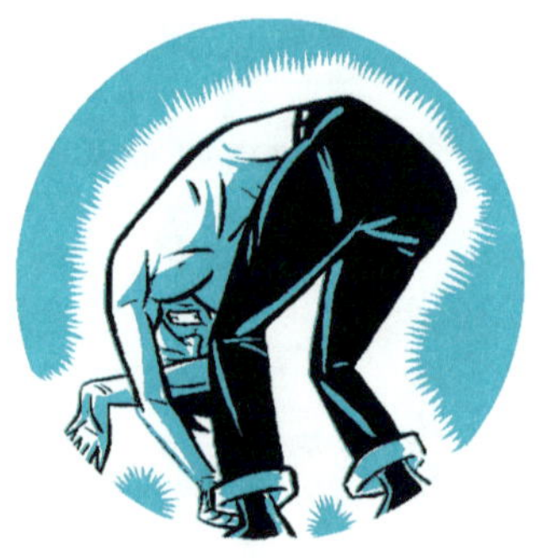

JUNKSICK AND ON THE STREET

My girlfriend saw me too often lying on the bathroom floor enveloped by porcelain and emitting low frequency moans that scared the cats back. She enlisted help and threw me onto St Lawrence street at 1 a.m. one Friday. When I rolled out from the car and onto the street I looked around seeing only the healthy disgusted looks of passers by and I think I told them to fuck off but maybe that was in my head. I try horizontal and it's shaky and only inspires my stomach to finally empty the contents of three past and prosperous day's food onto the side of a parked car in a colorful stream — it feels so good to have that out. I'm in my own world now and to hide I slide into shadows to be seamless in the background of life while looking for money. What you want is what you get but I wanted a whole lot more.

I head straight to Amhearst to get fucked by Jean Francois. He doesn't care what I smell or look like as long as I have a hole to pierce. He lingers and I'm so sick and my ass hurts that way I hate and I crawl from sweat and skin, taking his money and claw on the door of my dealer. I fall in and he hits me up in a divine act of understanding. He makes me tea and I fall asleep watching Charlie's Angels.

Every day I think about killing myself but I hate melodrama; I've never wanted anyone's sympathy, it's all about obsessions and needs, desires and yearnings that I am never aware of. My whole life has been about altering my reality. Plastic surgery for the soul. It still hasn't worked.

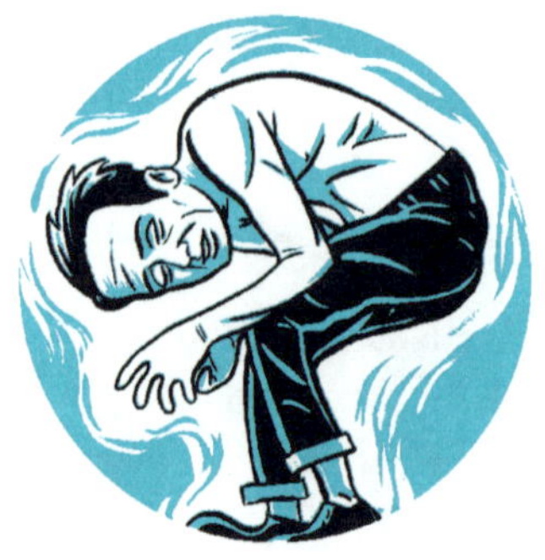

TREATMENT

My first counselor with the beautiful long long long legs that crossed

creating quivering sensations in my long-lost sex drive — only she

could arouse a dead man. Beyond that she cited cigarettes as equiv-

alents to heroin but she didn't know a fucking thing, God bless her

legs, so I went on resealing my libido in the sexless cast of heroin

knowing that people don't really understand unless they've done

junk at some time. It's a love affair higher than love and is not so

easy to disengage from. I went to treatment in northern Quebec

that had a pedophile priest — Andre the fag — and an ex-junkie —

Johnny Doper — in charge but both so out of control that after three weeks I convinced Johnny to pile his shit-heap car with donation money and drive to Montreal where we undid positivity by jamming coke and junk into our brains for a week straight until I ODed again and was left for dead. I managed again to pull out of it with sheer determination to get more dope and after four more hazy lazy years I found my treatment in Ottawa. Frank opened the door — the original drugstore cowboy who was bigger and smarter and funnier than anyone and somehow, especially after realizing you can't con a con, I let him reguide my energy to years of clean living and my ability to write this shit down.

Frank knew even my slightest lies and was compassionate without being a sucker. He held me on that thin line I needed to be on long enough to truly see my ways. He taught me through relating his own experiences and sharing his every intimacy every humiliation every thrill. He never said junk was bad, just that he got bad on junk, and that's the truth it ain't the drug that kills, it's too beauti-

ful to do any harm, but when it marries itself to insane self–hating

brains it forms the concoction of desperate willing-to-kill junkies

that lose reality — usually forever.

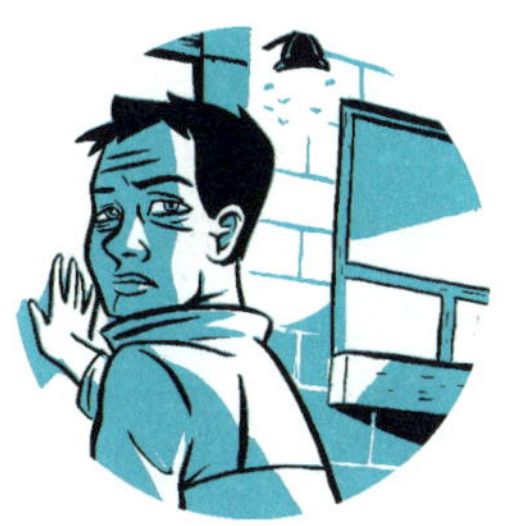

When John L'Ecuyer burst on the Canada's indie film scene three years ago with **Curtis' Charm**, it was immediately apparent that he was no stranger to the funky, desolate environment of heroin users evoked in the script. Like Jim Carroll, whose short story he had adapted for his first feature, L'Ecuyer clearly had the inside track on the way junkies talked, ate, hung out and made peace with their lives. A tale of magic, betrayal and death, **Curtis' Charm** could easily have descended into bathos or, more disastrously, into a didactic evocation of the evils of smack. In L'Ecuyer's hands, it came off as a funny and sad look at two friends trying to work out a situation that was beyond their control.

Meeting L'Ecuyer at that time, it was easy to see that here was an artist who had more than his career in mind while making a film. Though a private person in many ways, John was open to talking about his time as an addict in Montreal. He had spent nearly a decade scuffling through the Montreal underground, a junked-out denizen of the one Canadian city with a history of wayward nocturnal pleasures. Besides **Curtis' Charm**, he had directed **UseOnceAndDestroy**, an intense and poetic short which evoked his harrowing and beautiful past in Montreal. While he had moved away from the devastating junkie life, L'Ecuyer was using his art to work through the events that had transfixed him from adolescence to adulthood.

He has continued that project since that time, expanding on the reminisces of his past friendships in Montreal. **UseOnceAndDestroy** now exists on CD as a self-described "crime funk soundtrack of the street." Composed by Chris Byrne and Sean Turrell with lyrics by L'Ecuyer, it features a techno-bluesy sound-wash with appropriately cool vocal stylizings. You are now holding the book, parts of which appear in two early short films, **Lowlife** (on Harvey) and **UseOnceAndDestroy** (the first three chapters) and in L'Ecuyer's recent documentary, **Confessions of a Rabid Dog**.

While researching that film, which chronicles the varying experiences of a disparate group of ex-junkies, L'Ecuyer spent time in the Montreal which he has loved and lost. He discovered that "there's only three or four people from my old circle of users who are still alive. Pretty much they are like scattered detritus. It's a little hard to look at that sometimes because I saw a lot of those people when they were teenagers, when they just started using, and there was still that sheen of youthfulness in their eyes and face and skin."

One survivor from that period helped reconnect him with recent ex-users in Montreal. Her help and the assistance of Peter Kunst and Frank Prendergast from Ottawa's James Street Recovery Program proved instrumental in acquainting L'Ecuyer with a new group of self-aware addicts who are in the process of staying clean from hard drugs. L'Ecuyer rehabilitated himself at James Street and is a believer in their system in which former junkies are the counselors for the recently detoxed patients. "Ex-heroin addicts can call a con a con," observes L'Ecuyer. "A social worker might say, 'I think you're lying,' to someone while an ex-addict is such a practiced liar that it is easy (for him or her) to say, 'I know you're bullshitting me because I've told the same lie.'"

L'Ecuyer made **Confessions of a Rabid Dog** in order to get to "the heart of a heroin addict. I know that sounds poetic but it is really practical. I was trying to understand what was the thing that made us snap and start thinking that heroin's OK." Eschewing the traditional documentary format in which an outsider clinically analyzes an exotic subject, L'Ecuyer injects himself into the film. Using some of the text entitled **My Story** from this book, he delineates episodes from his own addiction. Shot in an interpretative style by Harald Bachman, L'Ecuyer and Ben Mazzotta, who was also the cameraman on **UseOnceAndDestroy**, L'Ecuyer's confessional sequences comprise the most impressive moments in the film.

Starting with his films from 1995, L'Ecuyer has succeeded in creating two trilogies centered on his experiences with drug culture. **UseOnceAndDestroy** is now available in three formats, as a CD, a film short and a book. And the films **Curtis' Charm**, **Confessions of a Rabid Dog** and **UseOnceAndDestroy** which articulate aspects of that life employ different formal strategies: the first being a narrative feature, the second, a personal documentary and the third, an experimental short. Regarding the differing intents, L'Ecuyer acknowledges that "the book is really about my loving certain people and how touched I was by interacting with them, the feature is about friendship and faith and the documentary is about trying to understand what is really at the heart of any person who decides consciously or subconsciously to become a heroin addict."

What is most striking about L'Ecuyer is his absolute refusal to condemn heroin addiction. "I loved those people I used to use with. I was living in a society where I was immersed in it. It wasn't really about heroin. I didn't go out with these people and say, 'let's talk about heroin, let's talk about the chemical makeup of heroin.' It was really a subculture and within that subculture, the width and breadth of all emotional experiences were played out." The human dimensions of heroin addicts have rarely been as well delineated as in these works by John L'Ecuyer.

Marc Glassman *is a radio and print journalist, film curator and editor for* ***Take One*** *magazine. He is the proprietor of* ***Pages****, a Toronto bookshop and the editor of the* ***Pages Books*** *imprint for* ***Gutter Press****.*

Thanks to Chantal, Mike C, the brothers Gerry (Gerald to you) and Mike, Sandra (Dylan Thomas) and Alicja, Marc Glassman for understanding this book, Gus Van Sant for helping, Geoff Pevere, Jane Fransisco for being the first to publish my stories, Jenny and Crazy Sam, VENUE, MATRIX and Pills a go-go, Wendy Kennish, Charlotte Mickie, Mark Asquith and Carolyn Bennett for 'championing' the film based on this text, Chris Byrne for 'championing' the CD based on this text, Charlotte Rose for believing in me, Patti Seaman, Stephen Reid, Susan Musgrave, David McIntosh, Frank Prendergast and Peter Kunst for rehabilitating me, Mary Pie and Ted for diagnosing me right, The Cafe Santropol for patience, compassion and understanding above and beyond...

Made with the assistance of the Toronto Arts Council.

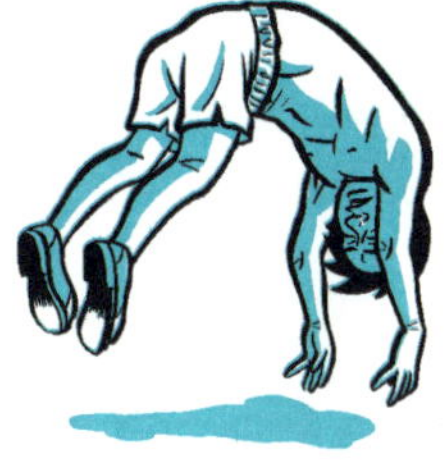